Flatten YOUR Stomach

Ann Dugan and the editors of Consumer Guide®

Thorsons

An Imprint of HarperCollins*Publishers*

Thorsons
An Imprint of HarperCollins*Publishers*
77–85 Fulham Palace Road,
Hammersmith, London W6 8JB

Published by Thorsons 1988
17   19   20   18

© Publications International Ltd 1985
© Patrick Stephens Ltd 1988
© Thorsons Publishers Ltd 1988

Ann Dugan asserts the moral right to
be identified as the author of this work

A catalogue record for this book
is available from the British Library

ISBN 0 7225 1857 9

Printed in Great Britain by
Woolnough Bookbinding Ltd
Irthlingborough, Northamptonshire

CONTENTS

Special Note

As with any exercise programme, you should consult your doctor before you start. If you have any special problems, such as being overweight, diabetic or if you suffer from a specific illness, or drink or smoke heavily, you should discuss plans fully with your doctor before you start.

THE FLATTEN YOUR STOMACH PROGRAMME

You can stay trim and shapely—no matter what age you are. While it is true that many physical changes occur through a woman's life, you can continue to look and feel young and healthy. The proper fitness plan can help you retain or maintain a firm, youthful figure

The Flatten Your Stomach Programme is a fast, effective exercise plan designed especially for women. With the Flatten Your Stomach Programme, you can shape and tone your muscles, control your weight, and build the strength and energy you need to meet demands of a busy, active life.

Shaping the Stomach

If you have been exercising and watching your diet, but your stomach still is not flat, you have been working on the wrong programme. There are four abdominal muscles, which act like a natural girdle. Their purpose is to hold in and support all the organs contained in the abdominal cavity. They do this with very little support from the bones in the trunk. If this natural girdle does not remain strong and tight, the muscles become even weaker, the internal organs slip and press against the abdominal wall, gravity pulls the abdomen lower and lower, and a protruding stomach results. That is why you need a balanced exercise programme to trim and tone all the muscle layers that mold and shape the stomach.

The Flatten Your Stomach Programme works because it

exercises all four sets of muscles in the stomach area. It also alternates dense muscle contractions with stretching exercises so that there is a complete balance of strength and tone of all the stomach muscles. These muscles usually respond rapidly to a well-designed exercise plan. After just a few weeks with the Flatten Your Stomach Programme, you'll be amazed at the difference in the way you look and feel.

Following The Programme

The Flatten Your Stomach Programme consists of warm up exercises, muscle toning exercises for the stomach area, and cool down exercises. The stomach flattening exercises are divided into three levels: Beginning, Intermediate, and Advanced. Always start your workout with the Warm Up and end it with the Cool Down, regardless of what level you are working on in the stomach flattening exercises.

The Warm Up helps your body to ease into more vigorous activity and lessens your chances of being injured. A good warm up raises your body's internal temperature and stimulates the movement of oxygen and blood in the body. The warm up also contains stretches to maintain flexibility in the joints and to prevent injury to the ligaments and tendons around the joints. Do the stretching movements slowly, in a controlled fashion. Avoid fast, jerky movements which could result in injury to the joints or tearing of the muscle fibres.

Always end the session with the Cool Down. These exercises help return the body to the pre-exercise state. They gradually restore blood circulation and breathing to normal rates, thus preventing weakness, lightheadedness and dizziness. They also help reduce muscle stiffness after exercise. Do not neglect these exercises. The Cool Down is an important part of the programme.

How To Use The Programme

No matter what your present level of fitness may be, start with the Beginning Programme. Then gradually work your way up through to the Intermediate and Advanced Programmes. The number of times you should repeat each exercise is indicated in the exercise instructions. If the number of repetitions indicated seems too difficult, do fewer repetitions to start. You can gradually add more repetitions as you build up strength. Never push yourself to the point of strain or injury. Start slowly and work at a pace that is comfortable for you.

Here are guidelines for working your way through the programme from the Beginning level up through the Intermediate and Advanced levels.

Beginning Programme

When you first start this exercise programme your workout should consist of the following:
1.   Do all of the exercises in the Warm Up.
2.   Do 6 exercises of your choice from the Beginning Programme.
3.   Do all of the exercises in the Cool Down.
As your strength and endurance increases, gradually add more exercises each week until you can easily complete all the exercises in the Beginning Programme (in addition to the Warm Up and Cool Down).

Intermediate Programme

When the entire Beginning Programme becomes easy to

do (usually after about 4 to 6 weeks), start the Intermediate Programme as follows:
1. Do all of the exercises in the Warm Up.
2. Do 10 exercises of your choice from the Intermediate Programme.
3. Do all of the exercises in the Cool Down.
Then gradually add more exercises each week until you can easily complete all of the exercises in the Intermediate Programme at the number of repetitions indicated (in addition to the Warm Up and the Cool Down).

Advanced Programme

When the entire Intermediate Programme becomes easy for you, go on to the Advanced Programme as follows:
1. Do all of the exercises in the Warm Up.
2. Do 10 exercises of your choice from the Advanced Programme.
3. Do all of the exercises in the Cool Down.
Gradually add exercises each week until you are doing all of the exercises in the Advanced Programme at the number of repetitions indicated in the instructions (along with the Warm Up and Cool Down). You can continue to work on the Advanced Programme indefinitely to maintain the fitness level you have achieved.

In the beginning, your workout may take about 20 minutes to complete, since you will be doing fewer exercises. As you add more exercises, the workout should last about 40 minutes to receive the most benefit from the programme.

When you first begin the Flatten Your Stomach Programme, it is recommended that you work out 3 days a week, alternating exercise days with days of rest. As you advance, work up to exercising 5 days a week. Establish a routine and stick to it. Make exercise an essential part of your life.

If you are off the programme for any length of time, go back and start with the Beginning Programme, and again work up slowly to the Advanced Programme. Remember, it takes only 72 hours for the body to start losing its strength and endurance! So once you get started, keep with it.

The Target Heart Rate Range

The Warm Up and the first group of standing exercises in each programme are aerobic exercises. That means that they condition the heart and lungs, as well as the stomach muscles. Through aerobic exercise, you are increasing your heart rate, strengthening the heart muscle, burning off excess fat, and raising the internal body temperature to prepare for the rest of the workout.

When you exercise, your heart should be beating at 70 to 85 percent of its maximum rate for your age group. This 70 to 85 percent of your maximum heart rate is called the 'training range' or 'target heart rate range'. If your heart range is below the target range during exercise you're not sufficiently challenging your heart and circulatory system. If it is above the target heart rate, you're challenging it too much, and you should pause briefly to rest until the heart rate returns to the target heart rate range. To find out if you're in the 'target heart rate range,' stop after the warm up, and take your pulse.

To take your pulse, place your first two fingers on the inside of your wrist just below your thumb. Count the number of beats for 10 seconds. Then multiply that by 6 to determine your pulse rate per minute. Consult the chart in this section to see if your heart rate is within the the recomended training range. If it is within range continue working. Then take the pulse again 15 to 20 minutes later.

Notice that the training rate will improve as you advance through the programme. However, do *not* try to attain the target heart rate when you first start the programme, and do *not* try to work up to it too quickly. Take the resting heart rate before beginning exercise and again 10 minutes after finishing the workout. The pulse should return to normal (the approximate beginning resting heart rate) by that time.

Training Heart Rates*
To Determine the Conditioning Effects of Exercise

Age	Beats in 10 seconds		Beats in 1 minute	
	Minimum 70%	Maximum 85%	Minimum 70%	Maximum 85%
35	21	26	126	156
40	21	26	126	156
45	21	25	126	150
50	20	24	120	144
55	19	23	114	138
60	19	23	114	138
65	18	22	108	132
70	17	21	102	126

*These figures are averages for healthy individuals. For exact figures for yourself, ask your doctor. If your age falls between the ages shown in the chart, follow the averages for the age higher than your own age. Note that with training, cardiovascular efficiency and strength changes very little with aging.

Setting Your Goals

Although it is commonly said that your waist should measure 10 inches less than your bust and 12 inches less than your hips, this is an ideal only. We are individuals. Each person's body is different in structure, heredity, age and metabolism. Even stress can add 2 inches to your waist at times, due to increased pressure and water retention. Therefore, before you begin, analyze your body in regard to these factors. Then you can set a realistic goal for attaining the trim, tight waist and firm, flat abdomen you want.

Body Structure

To determine your bone structure, measure around the wrist at the wrist bone. If the measure is 5 inches, you have small bones; 5½ inches, medium bones; and 6 inches, large bones. If the bones are large, naturally you will tend to weigh more than a smallboned person.

As you stand, take a deep breath. The distance from the last rib to the top of the hip bone should be roughly 4 to 6 inches. If the measure is less, the muscles at the sides of the waistline will be shorter and thicker. Pregnancy tends to seperate the rib cage and pelvic structure, making the abdominal area wider. Pregnancy also stretches the muscles and skin in this area, particularly if you have had a large baby or were pregnant in your teens or early twenties when the muscles weren't fully developed or strengthened. Stomach muscles can also be weakened as a result of surgery.

Heredity

You may have been born with a tendency to accumulate fatty tissue, due to an overabundance of fat cells in the body. Since this is inherited, these fat cells can remain with you for life; they can even expand to more fatty tissue, if the diet is not restricted early in life. Exercise burns the fat in these cells so that it does not accumulate in excessive amounts, particularly in the stomach area.

Age

Each decade after the age of 25, we lose about 3 to 5 percent of our muscle mass. And muscle is often replaced by fatty tissue if we don't exercise. Muscle strength may decrease 40 percent by the age of 55, depending upon the physical demands of our occupations and leisure activities. The muscle strength loss is proportionately slower in women, since women tend to remain more active throughout life.

In most areas of the body, there is little change in measurement, except in the stomach area. While there is generally only a 6 to 16 percent increase in men, there is usually a 25 to 35 percent change in women. Therefore, exercise is one of the most important prescriptions for maintaining firm, strong stomach muscles. Exercise keeps the muscle fibres dense and in tone. This means that less muscle tissue degenerates, and less muscle is replaced with connective tissue and fat.

In addition to muscular change, there are changes in the

skeletal system. The bones themselves become denser and heavier. This is particularly true in the chest area, where the breastbone becomes heavier and is harder to hold up. This leads to drooping or round shoulders, which automatically causes bulging of the stomach muscles. A gradual wearing away of the discs in the spine also leads to back pain, unless the stomach and back bones are strong enough to support the spine.

A weak back and weak stomach muscles go hand in hand. If the stomach muscles are weak, the internal organs slip and press against the abdominal wall. As the organs progressively slip, the muscles progressively weaken and the stomach protrudes even more. The stomach muscles become too weak to hold the hips in place, which throws the body posture out of alignment. The vertebrae of the spine are squeezed together, putting pressure on the nerves in the area. The result is low back pain.

There have been many suggested 'cures' for back pain. But the most widely prescribed remedy is this: exercise properly to strengthen the stomach and back muscles. Therefore, an added benifit of the Flatten Your Stomach Programme is the conditioning effect if will have on your back.

Metabolism

The basic metabolic rate—the rate at which we use energy—decreases slightly but steadily through adult life. This means we are burning fewer calories in our daily routines. Individual bodies work at different rates depending on age, sex, size, heredity and physical activity. Muscle tissue uses up more energy than body fat does. Since males have a higher percentage of muscle, most males are blessed with faster metabolic rates than are females.

What can you do? Physical activity is the only prescription for increasing the metabolic rate. And once it is raised, it takes many hours to return to the normal state. Regular, strenuous exercise results in a metabolism that continues to burn more calories (even in your sleep).

Come Alive!

Once you analyze yourself and understand these normal changes in your body, forget your chronological age. Instead take a positive approach and enter a new phase of living. You can roll back the years and return to the figure, vitality, and spirit of youth. Stating your age in years does not accurately describe your appearance, vigour, or life expectancy. It does not indicate the health of the bones, strength of the heart, vital lung capacity, muscular endurance, skin elasticity and hormonal functioning. Testing these factors would reveal your true or physiological age. At age of 40 or 50, you may have a physiological age of only 20 or 30. By following the exercise plan in this book, as well as a sound nutritional programme, you can have the slender, firm, youthful, healthy body you want.

Combine Exercise with Good Nutrition

Along with this exercise programme, watch what you eat. Select a variety of foods from from each of the four basic food groups, and eat moderate portions. Since all foods can be converted into body fat, the amount of food you consume, your energy intake, must be less than or equal to the amount of energy you expend. The scales must balance. If not you will have an excess of fat. This sounds simple, but as we all know it is not. Psychological factors affect the amounts and kinds of food we eat as well as how our bodies use food for nourishment. Food habits do not 'just happen.' They are gradually developed from childhood, and they are not easily changed. The first step is to analyze your daily nutrition. Nutrition—a well-balanced diet every day—does make a difference. A women with a well-nourished body has the best chances of maintaining beauty, youth, and vitality throughout life.

Is That Fat or Is It Bloat?

Puffy eyes, swollen hands and ankles, a bloated stomach —water retention is usually the cause. Millions of women experience water retention on a regular basis, sometimes causing a weight gain of 2 or 3 pounds overnight. Sometimes headaches, fatigue, and irritability accompany this bloating. If you are concerned see a doctor. But the commonest type of water retention is not serious. In most cases, the kidneys activate certain hormones that make the body retain salt and water. Eventually there is a buildup of water in the tissues. The exact cause is not known, but many doctors suspect that the female hormone oestrogen may make the body retain salt. The sodium in salt helps retain water. When you experience bloating, exercise can help. Exercise forces the fluids from the tissues and keeps the blood circulating, preventing the pooling of blood and fluids. To help relieve bloating:

● Cut down on salt.(This is especially important for women with hypertension.)

● Elevate the legs, particularly late in the day.

● Wear support stockings.

● Do not cross the legs when sitting.

● Exercise regularly. Many of the exercises in the Flatten Your Stomach Programme are especially helpful in relieving bloating.

Programme Guidelines

1. It is recommended that you consult your doctor before beginning this or any other exercise programme.
2. If you have not been exercising regularly or if you have a medical history that would limit activity, consult your doctor as to which exercise in this programme is best for you.
3. Wear comfortable clothing so that your movements are not restricted.
4. Wear an athletic shoe or a firm support shoe that will absorb shock to the ankles, knees and back.
5. While exercising, breathe normally. Do not hold the breath or use controlled or forced breathing.
6. Avoid dizziness by pausing briefly before changing direction.
7. Stop exercising if you feel dizzy or nauseated.
8. Start slowly, doing the number of repetitions indicated in the exercise instructions (or fewer). Then work up gradually to do more repetitions.
9. Eat only in moderation during the two hours before you exercise; otherwise nausea could occur.
10. Try to do the programme at the same time each day you work out so that you establish a routine. The time of day you exercise is not important. Choose a time that's best for you, and stick to your routine.
11. Do not expect to be of equal strength or vigor each day. Some days you may be more up to it.
12. Do not overstress yourself. Work to the point of fatigue—not to the point of exhaustion, strain or injury.
13. Monitor your heart by checking your pulse throughout the programme. Also watch for signs of stress, strain or injury.
14. Some soreness can be expected at first since you are using muscles that you may not have exercised for some

time.

15. Supplement this programme with as much recreational physical activity as possible, such as golf, swimming, or walking.

16. Form is critical. Try to do the exercises exactly as indicated.

17. Use a mat, thick carpet, or folded towel when doing the floor exercises to avoid rubbing or irritation to the coccyx (tailbone).

18. Notice that some of the exercises instruct you to keep thefeet flat (not pointed). The purpose of this is to condition and lengthen the hamstring muscles in the back of the legs. It also makes the pull on the stomach muscles stronger.

19. Notice that some exercises instruct you to clasp your hands behind the head (not behind the neck). This is to prevent the head from bobbing, which would place undue stress on the neck.

Exercise!

Medical authorities believe that exercise may be the single most effective way to improve the length and quality of life. We were designed to be active. So go to it! No matter what shape you are in now or what age you are, you can improve and achieve dramatic results through exercise. You can look and feel better than you ever have before.

For a new, trimmer and fitter you
the exercise programme begins
here.

SWEEP

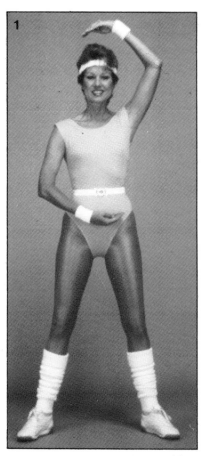

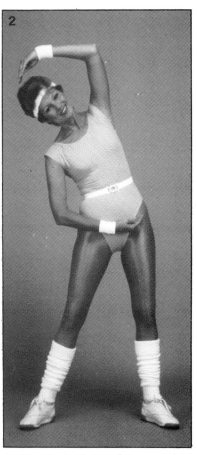

1 Stand with the feet wide apart, knees slighty bent, arms curved in arcs with the left arm up, right arm down.

2 Bend to the right, pressing the left arm to the right. Change arm positions, with the right arm up and left arm down, and lean to the left. Continue in a swinging, flowing movement alternately leaning right and left. Do 25 times.

FLOW THROUGH

1 Stand with the feet wide apart, knees slightly bent, both arms to the right side.

2 Bend the knees, and swing both arms down in front.

3 Swing the arms up to the left, straighten the knees, and turn the head and shoulders to the left. Using the same motion, swing the arms and the body back to the right side. Do 25 times alternately swinging left and right.

BACK STRETCH

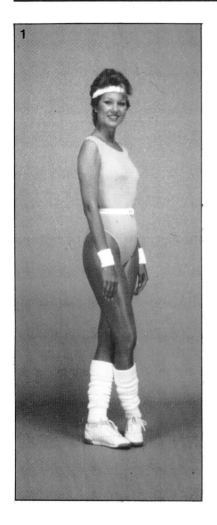

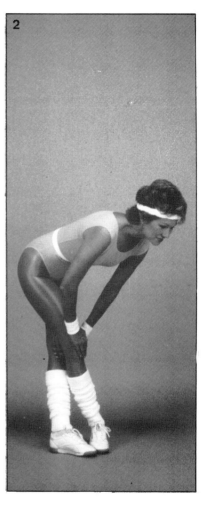

1 Stand with the feet crossed, toes turned in, hands at the sides.

2 Slowly bend from the waist, place the hands on the knees, flatten the back, and lift the head. Hold this position for 5 to 10 counts.

AEROBIC RUN

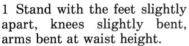

1 Stand with the feet slightly apart, knees slightly bent, arms bent at waist height.

2 Run in place, kicking the legs up high in back. At the same time, clap the hands in time to the movement. Run for 1 minute. Gradually work up to 6 minutes. You should be breathing more heavily after this run.

Check your pulse immediately after this exercise. Consult the introduction to this book to see if you are attaining your correct 'target heart rate' range.

KICK UP

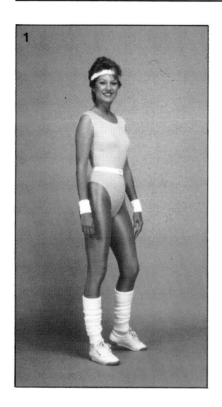

1 Stand with the weight on the right leg, left leg slightly to the side with the weight on the toes, arms at the sides.

2 Raise the left leg forward and up as high as possible. At the same time, swing both hands forward and try to touch the left ankle. Return to the starting position. Do 8 times with each leg.

WAISTLINE WHITTLER

1 Stand with the weight on the right leg, left knee bent and turned to the side with the weight on the toes, left hand on the hip, right arm at the side.

2 Keeping the knee turned out, raise the left leg as high as possible. At the same time extend the right arm and lean toward the right. Return to the starting position. Do 8 times with each leg.

LEAN

1 Stand with the feet wide apart, knees slightly bent, hands clasped behind the head.

2 Bend the left knee to the side and lean the torso to the left. Return to the starting position, and repeat to the right side. Do 10 times, alternating left and right.

THE BOXER

1 Stand with the feet wide apart, right hand on the hip, left arm bent up with the hand in a fist.

2 Bend the right knee, and extend the left arm across the body to the right. Return to the starting position. Do 10 times with each arm.

TOUCH UP

1 Stand with the weight on the right leg, left leg to the side with the weight on the toes, right hand behind the head, left hand on the hip.

2 Bend the left knee up toward the chest, and touch the right elbow to the knee. Return to the starting position. Do 10 times with each leg.

HURDLER'S CIRCLE

1 Sit in a hurdler's position with the left leg bent back, right leg extended to the side, hands on the floor at the sides.

For any exercise that requires kneeling, sitting, or lying on the floor, do the exercise on a mat, a thick carpet, or a folded towel.

2 Raise the right leg, and circle it 10 times. Reverse the leg positions, and circle the left leg 10 times.

You are working the transverse abdominal muscles, which crisscross the abdominal area, Tightening these muscles really flattens the stomach.

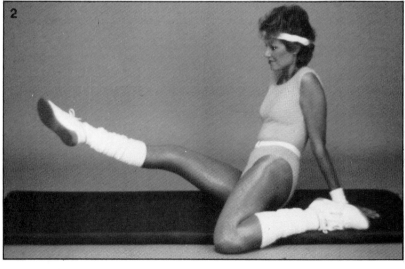

A TOUGH ACT

1 Sit with the legs apart, knees bent, feet flat on the floor, arms folded across the chest.

2 Slowly lower the back to the floor keeping the shoulders and head up off the floor.

3 Sit up and swing the left leg out to the side. Return to the starting position. Do 8 times with each leg.

This is a good exercise for firming the lower abdomen

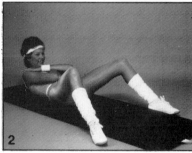

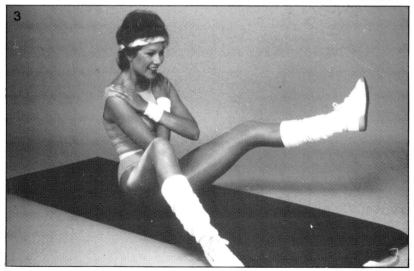

LIFT UP

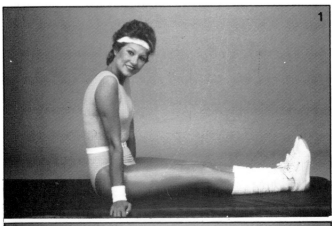

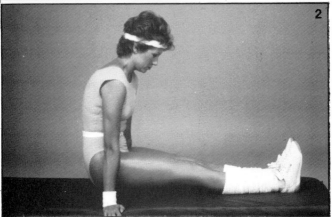

1 Sit on the floor with the legs extended forward, toes up hands on the floor at the hips.

2 Lift the hips, and pull in the stomach. Hold for 5 counts. Return to the starting position. Do 5 times.

Make sure you lift the hips straight up off the floor.

SIDELINE SQUEEZE

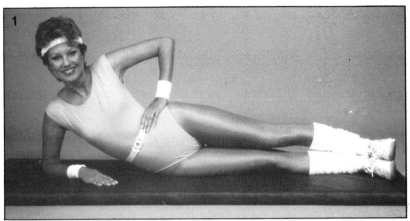

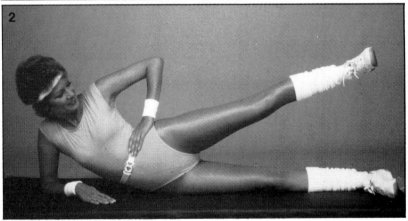

1 Lie on the right side on the floor with the legs extended, weight on the right elbow, left hand on the hip.

2 Keeping the foot flat (not pointed) raise the left leg up as high as posible. Lower the leg to the starting position. Do 10 times on each side.

Do not turn the leg; keep it in the side position.

SWING IT

1 Lie on the left side with the weight on the left elbow and right hand, both feet off the floor, right knee bent in toward the chest.

2 Extend the right leg forward.

3 Then swing the leg back. Bend the knee in again to return to the starting position. Do 10 times on each side.

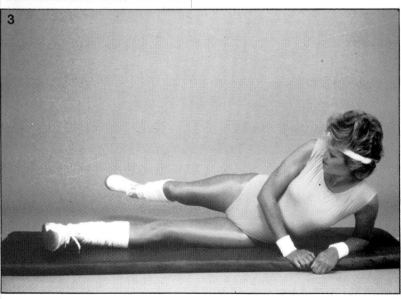

TWIST AND TOUCH

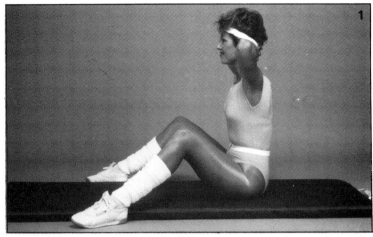

1 Sit with the feet wide apart, knees bent, feet flat on the floor, hands clasped behind the head.

2 Twist and touch the right elbow to the outside of the left knee. Return to the starting position. Repeat to the right side. Do 10 times, alternating left and right.

THE FLATTENER

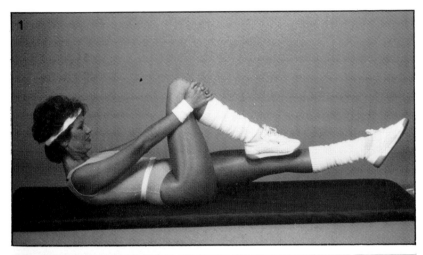

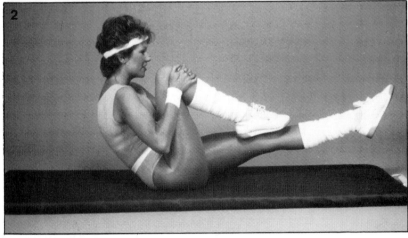

1 Lie on the back with the left leg off the floor and extended straight out, right foot on the left knee, hands holding the right knee, head up off the floor.

2 Gripping the knee, sit up. Return to the starting position. Do 8 times with each leg.

TRY HARDER

1 Sit with the weight on the hands, or the elbows, legs extended up, toes turned out to the sides.

2 Slowly lower the legs to the floor.

3 Bend the knees in towards the chest. Then extend the legs up to return to the starting position. Do 8 times.

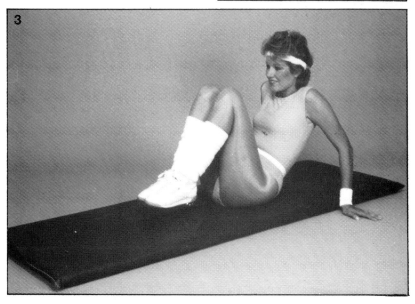

TONE UP

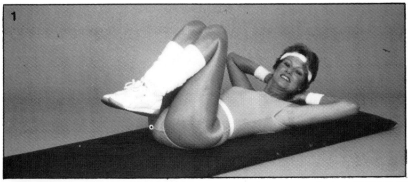

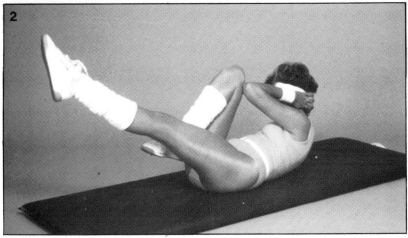

1 Lie on the back, hands clasped behind the head with the head off the floor, knees bent with the feet off the floor.

2 Pull the right knee in toward the chest, and touch the left elbow to the right knee. At the same time, extend the left leg straight out. Then touch the right elbow to the left knee, and extend the right leg. Do 10 to 15 times, alternating right and left.

OVERHEAD SWINGS

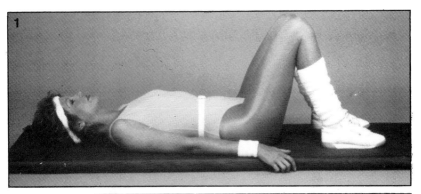

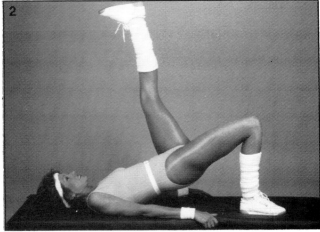

1 Lie on the back with the knees bent, feet flat on the floor, arms at the sides.

2 Lift the hips as high as possible. Then lift the left leg straight up. Hold for 5 counts. Return to the starting position. Do 3 times with each leg.

Do not lift the leg so high that you are placing pressure on the back of the neck. If you feel pain in the neck, stop doing this exercise.

41

COORDINATE IT

1 Stand with the weight on the right leg, left leg to the side with the weight on the toes, both arms extended to the right.

2 Bend the left knee up, and cross it to the right. At the same time, swing both arms down toward the left hip. Return to the starting position. Do 8 times with each leg.

DOUBLE DIP

1 Stand with the legs together, arms overhead.

2 Bend the knees, turn the torso to the right and touch the outside of the right knee with both hands. Return to the starting position. Do 10 times, alternating right and left.

43

FORWARD TOUCH-UP

1 Stand with the weight on the right foot, left leg to the side with the weight on the toes, left hand on the hip, right arm up.

2 Bend the left leg in front of the body, and touch the foot with the right hand. Return to the starting position. Do 10 times with each leg.

TURN IN

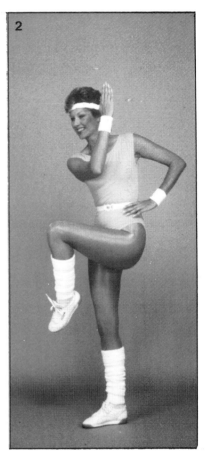

1 Stand with the feet wide apart, right arm out to the side, left hand on the hip.

2 Bend the right hand in toward the body (palm in front of the face). At the same time, bend the left knee up and across the body toward the right. Return to the starting position. Do 10 times with each leg.

45

THE LUNGE

1 Stand with the feet wide apart, arms at the sides.

2 Bend the right foot up in back. At the same time swing both arms up and to the left.

3 Lunge to the right side with the right foot, and swing both arms to the right. Return to the starting position. Do 8 times on each side.

KEEP ON TWISTING

1 Stand with feet wide apart, knees slightly bent, arms bent up at the sides, hands in fists.

2 Bend the left knee, and touch the right elbow to the knee. At the same time, twist the left arm up behind the back. Return to the starting position. Do 20 times, alternating right and left.

If you have a weak back, place one hand on the knee as you bend to support the back. Do the exercise only 8 times on each side, and do not alternate left and right.

SWEEP OVER

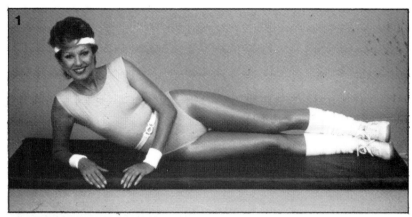

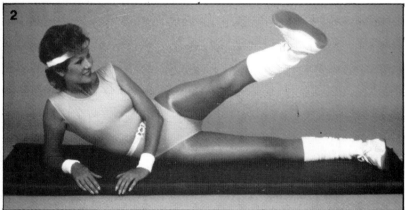

1 Lie on the right side with the legs extended, weight on the right elbow, left hand on the floor for support.

2 Keeping the foot flat, circle the left leg in a large sweeping movement 10 times. Turn over onto the other side, and circle the right leg 10 times.

SIDE LIFT

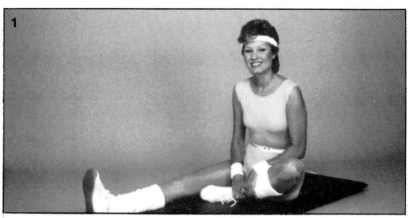

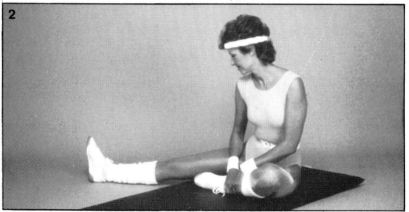

1 Sit on the floor with the left leg bent in, right leg extended forward, both hands holding the left angle.

2 Keeping the foot flat, raise the right leg, swing it to the side, and lower it to the floor. Lift the leg and return it to the starting position. Do 8 times with each leg.

This exercise is good for the transverse abdominal muscles, which crisscross the abdomen and can really hold in the stomach.

49

SIDE KICK

1 Sit with the feet wide apart, knees bent, feet flat on the floor, arms forward.

2 Kick the right leg out to the side. At the same time, swing both arms to the left. Return to the starting position. Do 8 times with each leg.

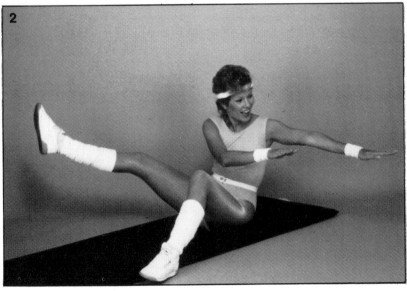

THE TABLE

1

1 Assume a 'gymnastic table' position, with the weight on the hands and right leg. Extend the left leg out to the side.

2 Raise the left leg up as high as possible. Then lower the leg to the floor at the side. Do 8 times with each leg.

2

51

CROSS KICK

1 Sit on the floor with the legs apart, arms extended out to the sides.

2 Raise the right leg, swing it across to the left side, and touch the right ankle with the left hand. Return to the starting position. Do 8 times with each leg.

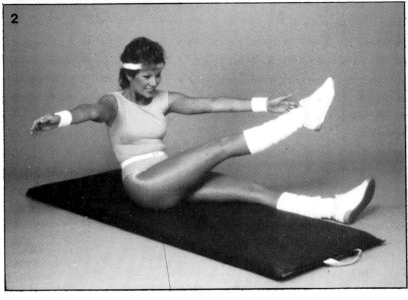

PRESS UP

1 Lie on the back with the weight on the elbows, knees bent, feet off the floor.

2 Press the body up by straightening the arms, and extend the legs out. Try to extend the legs as straight up as possible. You should feel the muscles contract around the rib cage. Return to the starting position. Do 5 times.

THE EXTENDER

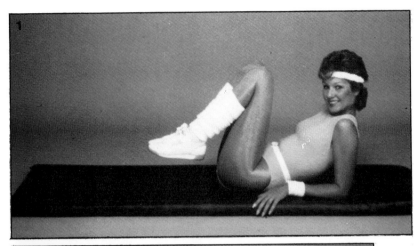

1 Sit with the weight on the elbows, knees bent in towards the chest, feet off the floor.

2 Extend the legs up and to the right. Bend the knees in toward the chest. Then extend the legs up and to the left. Do 15 times, alternating right and left.

54

CROSS SIT

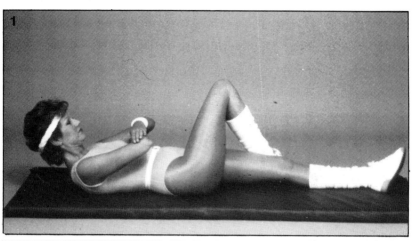

1 Lie on the back with the head up off the floor, hands holding the elbows. Extend the left leg, cross the right leg over the left so that the right foot is flat on the floor.

2 Keeping the legs in position on the floor, sit up and twist the folded arms to the right. Return to the starting position. Do 8 times. Then switch the leg positions, and do 8 times to the other side.

GRIP SIT

1 Lie on the back with the knees bent, feet flat on the floor and wide apart, heels as close as possible to the hips, head and shoulders off the floor, hands grasping the backs of the thighs.

2 Slowly sit up, keeping the feet on the floor. Return to the starting position. Do 10 times.

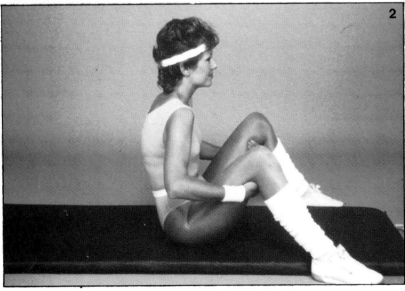

COMPRESS IT

1 Stand with the feet wide apart, arms out to the sides.

2 Swing the arms forward, and bend the right knee up toward the chest.

3 Then return the leg to the floor, bend the torso toward the floor, and press the arms up in back. Do 8 times with each leg.

This exercise compresses the stomach and helps eliminate bloating.

FIRM UP

1 Stand with the weight on the right leg, left leg slightly to the side with the weight on the toes, right hand behind the head, left hand on the hip.

2 Raise the left leg forward and up as high as possible, and touch the right elbow to the left knee. Return to the starting position. Do 8 times with each leg.

Great not only for the stomach but also for the back and hips.

CROSS OUT

1 Stand with the weight on the right leg, left leg to the side with the weight on the toes, body facing left, arms overhead.

2 Cross the left leg behind the right, bend from the waist, and swing both arms down toward the ankles. Try to touch the ankles with the hands. Return to the starting position. Do 8 times. Then do 8 more times, crossing the right leg behind the left.

DEEP BEND

1 Stand with the feet wide apart, knees slightly bent, arms bent up at the sides, hands in fists.

2 Lean the torso over the floor, bend the right knee, and touch the left elbow to the right calf. At the same time, twist the right arm up behind the back. Return to the starting position. Repeat to the other side. Do 10 to 20 times, alternating left and right.

CIRCLE AND SIT

1 Kneel with arms at the sides, hips resting on the heels.

2 Lifting the torso up, circle the arms up to the right.

3 Continue circling the arms up overhead, and then down to the left to return to the starting position. Repeat the circle pattern 8 times to the right, then 8 times to the left.

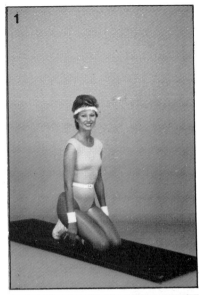

TOTAL TONE

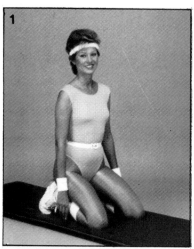

1 Kneel with the legs wide apart, arms at the side, hips resting on the heels.

2 Lift up the torso, put the right hand on the hip, and lean to the right. At the same time, extend the left leg to the side, and swing the left hand up and across to the right side. Return to the starting position. Do 8 times on each side.

Good not only for the waistline, but also for the inner thighs

CINCHER

1 Kneel on the right knee with the left leg extended straight forward, arms overhead.

2 Raise the left leg.

3 Then lower the leg to the floor. At the same time, press both hands to the floor on either side of the leg. Repeat 8 times with each leg.

Good not only for the stomach, but also for the backs of the thighs.

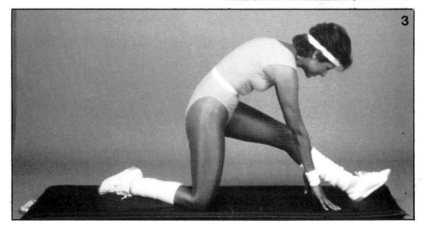

THE COMPLETE FEAT

1 Kneel with the legs wide apart, hips resting on the heels, hands on the floor behind the feet.

2 Raise the torso up off the heels, and press the left arm up and into the right side. Return to the starting position. Repeat to the other side. Do 8 times, alternating right and left.

Great for the stomach and inner thighs.

GO FOR IT

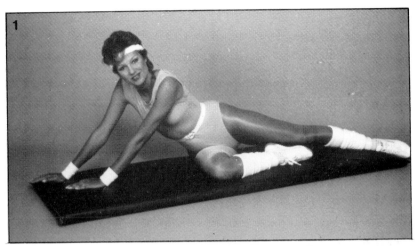

1 Sit with the right leg bent in front, left leg straight out to the side, both hands on the floor on the right side, body turned to the right.

2 Sit up, raise both arms and the left leg, and touch the left leg with both hands. Return to the starting position. Do 8 times on each side.

CHANGEOVER

1 Sit with the weight on the elbows, left leg extended out to the side, right leg straight up.

2 Keeping both elbows on the floor, cross the right leg over to touch the floor outside the left leg. Return to the starting position. Do 8 times with each leg.

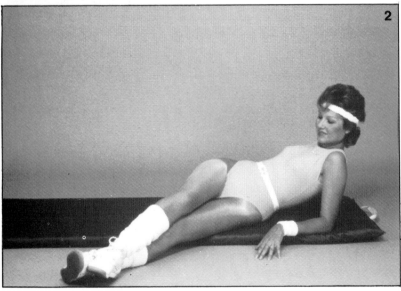

SUPER SIT

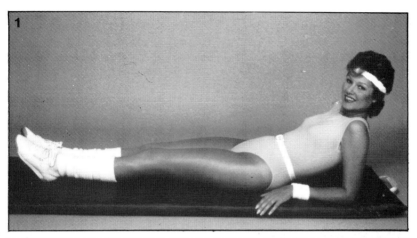

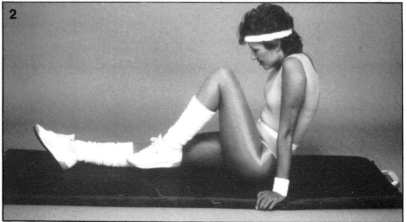

1 Lie with the weight on the elbows, hands at the hips, knees slightly bent, heels on the floor.

2 Press up to a sit by straightening the arms, press the chest forward, bend the left knee up to the chest, and bend the head towards the knee. Return to the starting position. Do 8 times with each leg.

SWING UP

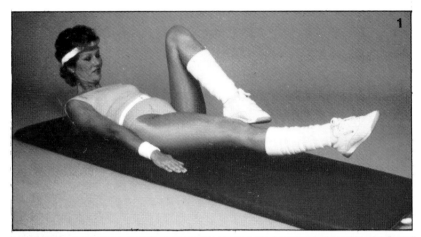

1 Lie with the arms at the sides, right leg extended and off the floor, left foot on the right knee, head up off the floor.

2 Keeping the legs in this position, sit up and swing the arms forward as far as possible. Return to the starting position. Do 8 times. Then reverse the leg positions, and do 8 more times.

TONE AND TIGHTEN

1 Lie with the right leg bent in front, left leg up, hands clasped behind the head. The head may be up off the floor or resting on the floor—whichever feels more comfortable for the back.

2 Slowly lower the left leg.

3 As it nears the other leg, swing the left leg out to the side. Then swing the left leg toward the centre, and return the leg up to the starting position. Do 8 times with each leg.

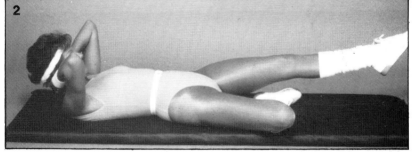

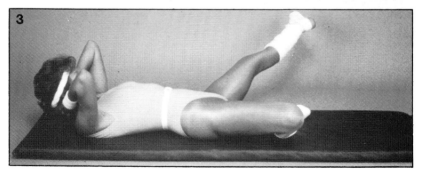

SIDE CIRCLES

1 Lie with the hands clasped behind the head, legs extended up. The head may be up off the floor or resting on the floor—whichever feels more comfortable for the back.

2 Circle the right leg to the side in a wide circle. Then circle the left leg. Circle each leg 15 to 20 times, alternating right and left.

Great for the muscles that crisscross the stomach.

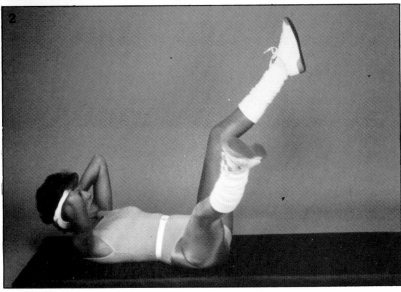

TABLE SET

1 Assume a 'gymnastic table' position, with the weight on the hands and right foot, hips up, left leg extended straight forward.

2 Swing the left leg to the left side. Return to the starting position. Do 8 times on each leg.

THE TILT

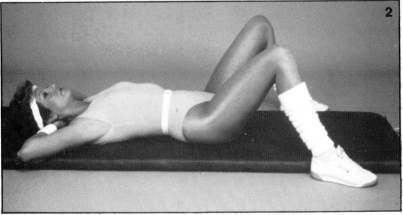

1 Lie on the back with the feet flat on the floor and wide apart, knees bent, head resting on the floor, hands clasped behind the head.

2 Pressing the back into the floor, lift the hips slightly off the floor.

Do not lift the hips too high, which would place too much pressure on the back of the neck.

72

DROP-OFF

1 Lie on the back, legs up, feet flat, hands clasped behind the head. The head may be up off the floor or resting on the floor —whichever feels more comfortable for the back.

2 Slowly lower the left leg to within a few inches of the floor. Hold for 5 counts. Bend the knee in toward the chest, and return the leg up to the starting position. Do 10 times with each leg.

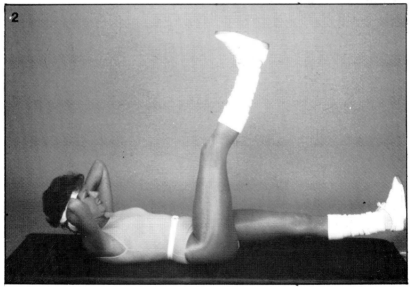

CRISSCROSS

1 Lie on the back with legs up and wide apart, hands clasped behind the head. The head may be up off the floor or resting on the floor—whichever feels more comfortable for the back.

2 Alternately cross the legs and then open the legs 10 times while gradually lowering the legs toward the floor and then raising them again to the starting position. For this exercise, point the toes (rather than keeping them flat).

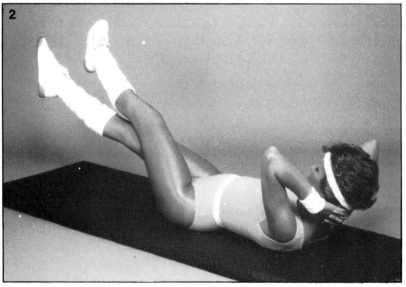

STRESS RELIEF

1 Kneel on the hands and knees with the head up.

2 Pull the right knee in toward the chest, clasp it with the right hand, and press the head down toward the knee. Hold for 5 counts. Repeat with the left knee. Do 3 times, alternating right and left.

This exercise strengthens the back and relieves stress on the back.

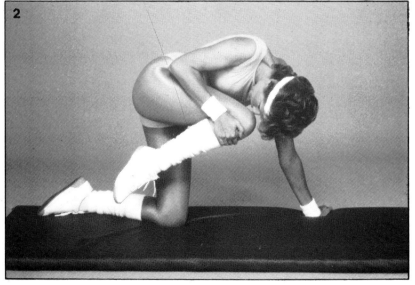

KNEE SWINGS

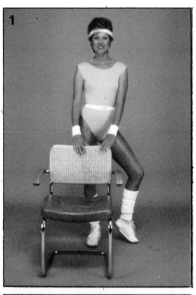

1 Stand facing the back of a sturdy chair, hands holding the back of the chair, weight on the right leg, left knee bent up with the weight on the toes.

2 Lift the left knee up to the side.

3 Then rotate the hips and turn the knee in front of the body to the right side. Return the knee to the starting position. Do 10 times with each leg.

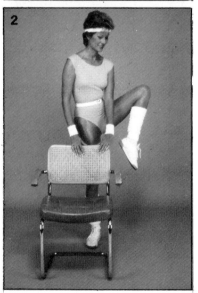

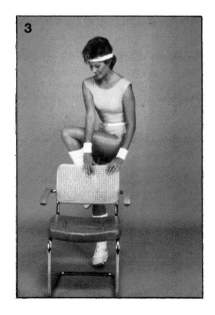

LEG SWINGS

1 Stand facing the back of a sturdy chair, hands holding the back of the chair, weight on the right leg, left leg to the side with the weight on the toes.

2 Keeping the left leg straight, lift it up as high as possible to the left side.

3 Then lower the leg and cross it in front of the body to the right side. Be careful not to hit the toes on the chair as the leg crosses. Swing each leg to the left and to the right 10 times.

This exercise is excellent for the waistline.

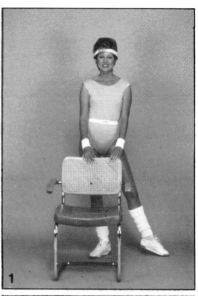

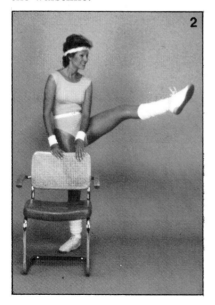

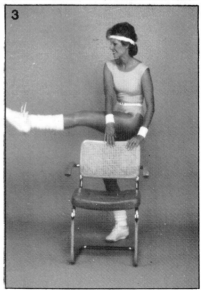

KICK OUT

1 Stand with the hands on the seat of a sturdy chair, gripping the sides of the chair, right knee bent up toward the chest.

2 Extend the right leg out in back, bending the leg up. Return to the starting position. Do 10 times for each leg.

Good for eliminating bloating.

THE ARCH

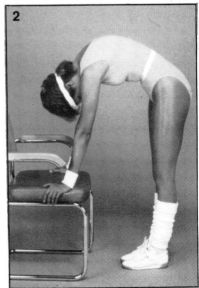

1 Stand with the hands on the seat of a sturdy chair, gripping the sides of the chair, with a flat back.

2 Push the hips forward, and round the back up as high as possible. Hold for 5 counts. Return to a flat back. Repeat 3 times.

Great for smoothing out wrinkly skin on the stomach.

Of further interest

SLIMMING YOUR HIPS AND THIGHS

Ann Dugan and the editors of Consumer Guide®

The most common figure complaints are in the area from the waist to the knees and this book, by concentrating on your hips and thighs, will help you get back into shape. This programme, one of the most effective yet designed, will help you feel slimmer, firmer and stronger, safely and without inducing injury or soreness. You will see and feel the results more rapidly than you would think possible. No matter how out of shape you may feel, these easy-to-follow routines will help to build a fitter you.